COMPLETE GUIDE IN TABLATURE AND STANDARD NOTATION

HOW TO PLAY
REGGAE
GUITAR
BY
RAY HITCHINS

HAL·LEONARD

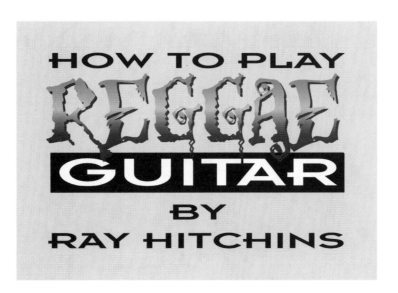

HOW TO PLAY REGGAE GUITAR

BY RAY HITCHINS

Photos by Louis Davis

Instrument Used: WRC Guitars

HAL•LEONARD CORPORATION

7777 W. BLUEMOUND RD. P.O. BOX 13819 MILWAUKEE, WI 53213

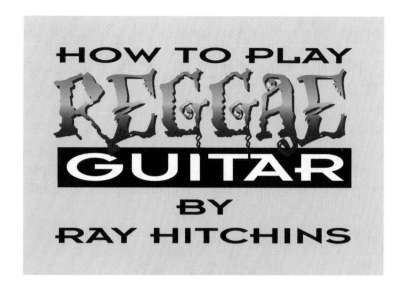

HOW TO PLAY REGGAE GUITAR BY RAY HITCHINS

CONTENTS

ACKNOWLEDGMENTS

I would like to thank the following people for their help and support, without which my work as a musician would not only be more demanding, but in many instances much less entertaining.

Eric Galletta at WRC guitars, Glyn Edwards and Pam O'Gorman for their technical recommendations, Mark Golding for his good advice, Peter Ashbourne, Desi Jones, and Peter Couch for their musical input. The artists and musicians with whom I have played over the years and have each offered me a learning experience in their own way. Ashley and Tina Prime for the many dinners and *Viz* magazines which I took advantage of; of course Mum and Dad; and last but never least Marie and Rachel, who provide a constant source of encouragement and inspiration.

Ray Hitchins

ABOUT THE AUTHOR

Ray Hitchins was born in the United Kingdom and started playing the guitar at the age of 12. His formative years were influenced by a wide variety of musical styles, including classical guitar, which he studied under Glyn Edwards and John Edwards. He is an associate of the London College of Music and besides teaching guitar, has worked as a session player in Germany and the United Kingdom during the late 1970s.

In 1981 he was offered a post as head of the Guitar department at the Jamaica School of Music in Kingston, Jamaica, where he worked for the next three years. Besides performing on T.V. and radio, he soon became a regular session player for local producers and eventually devoted all his time to free-lance work in the Kingston music scene. Over the years he has recorded and performed in the U.S.A., Canada, Mexico, Japan, and the Caribbean for artists such as Toots Hibbert, Barrington Levy, Dennis Brown, Borris Gardener, Marcia Griffiths, Tiger, Leroy Sibbles, Freddy McGregor, Alton Ellis, John Holt, Papa San, Carlene Davies, and Junior Tucker, to mention a few.

In 1988 he co-founded the group Skool, which became established as a leading backing band and performed as part of the Reggae Sunsplash world tour in 1992 and 1993. His production company, Crystal Cave Music Ltd., was formed in 1986 and is one of the major jingle production houses in Kingston, writing and producing music for products such as Pepsi, 7-Up, Heineken and Red Stripe beer.

INTRODUCTION

This book is based on experience gained over the last 10 years, living and working in Jamaica as a guitar teacher and free-lance player. During this time many changes have taken place in Reggae music, the greatest influence being the introduction of MIDI technology, with programmable and sequenced instruments. As a result, recording styles have changed drastically, and the average band, although not working in a studio as much, now has the added challenge of reproducing live what was created beat by beat on silicon chips.

This is not necessarily a bad thing, but the Reggae music that inspired me to write this book was, and still is, predominantly produced by a live rhythm section. The whole essence of Reggae is feel and where (in the measure) each instrument drops in relation to the beat. For anyone interested in this style, listening to the music of Bob Marley, Peter Tosh, Third World, and Toots Hibbert (to name a few) is a must. It is the best way to absorb the essential vibe that every Reggae musician needs.

What follows is intended to lay the groundwork for the potential Reggae guitarist and act as a formal introduction to this style and sound.

THE FUNDAMENTALS

YOUR EQUIPMENT

Before commencing with the technical exercises, consider the following points to ensure that you are equipped to produce a Reggae guitar sound.

Guitars

No hard-and-fast rules apply in the choice of guitars. The instrument should have good intonation and be capable of producing a fairly clean sound. If you are purchasing an instrument for the first time, I strongly recommend that you find an experienced guitarist who can advise you with your choice of instrument, and set up the instrument for your personal requirements.

String Action

Low action is not essential and, in extreme cases, can cause buzzes that hinder the production of a clean, bright sound. Many Reggae guitarists use relatively high action.

Pickups

The choice of pickups is a personal one. The standard pickups that most guitars are fitted with are adequate, providing they produce a strong clean signal.

String Gauge

The heavier the strings the less buzz they produce, but the harder they are to bend, and the more work they tend to require of the fingers! I recommend a light-gauge set, with a top E gauge of .010 and a bottom E gauge of .042. Always use a plain (unwound) third string (G).

Tone and Volume Controls

Make sure that both of these controls work effectively; they should not produce any abnormal electrical noises.

Picks

I recommend a medium-to-heavy pick, to produce a firm clean stroke in rhythm playing. The size and shape of the pick is a personal choice.

Amplifiers

An amplifier suitable for playing Reggae should be able to produce a clean, undistorted sound, with plenty of treble and middle tone variations, and have a built-in reverb unit. Many amplifiers are available with other useful built-in devices that can be used creatively in Reggae, but the criteria above are essential. Here is a typical amplifier setting that could be used:

(This is using a Peavey Studio Pro 40 and a Fender Stratocaster)

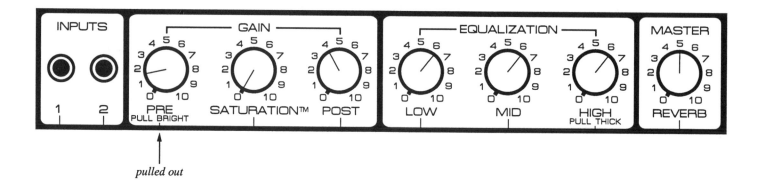

pulled out

Effects

The incorporating of mechanical and electronic effects into Reggae is, by tradition, fairly limited. Experiment with whatever is available to you, after you have mastered the basic techniques and feel.

RUDIMENTS

It is necessary to be familiar with the rudiments of music, especially simple rhythms, to be able to understand the exercises in this book.

The following are simple descriptions and names of notes and rests that you will be using. Study them carefully.

NOTE	EQUIVALENT REST	NAME
𝅝	▬	Whole Note
𝅗𝅥	▬	Half Note
♩	𝄽	Quarter Note
♪	𝄾	Eighth Note (Eighth notes when grouped together are written ♫)
𝅘𝅥𝅯	𝄿	Sixteenth Note (Sixteenth notes when grouped together are written 𝅘𝅥𝅰𝅘𝅥𝅰𝅘𝅥𝅰𝅘𝅥𝅰)

Important Points

1. All the exercises in this book have a $\frac{4}{4}$ time signature (four beats to each measure).

2. In a $\frac{4}{4}$ time signature a **Whole Note** represents *four beats*.

3. In a $\frac{4}{4}$ time signature a **Half Note** represents *two beats*.

4. In a $\frac{4}{4}$ time signature a **Quarter Note** represents *one beat*.

5. In a $\frac{4}{4}$ time signature a **Eighth Note** represents a *half beat*.

6. In a $\frac{4}{4}$ time signature a **Sixteenth Note** represents a *quarter beat*.

The above types of notes are counted as follows:

1. **The Whole Note**
   Count out loud while tapping out the note.

2. **The Half Note**
   Count out loud while tapping out the note.

3. **The Quarter Note**
   Count out loud while tapping out the note.

4. **The Eighth Note**
   Count out loud while tapping out the note.

5. **The Sixteenth Note**
   Count out loud while tapping out the note.

Here are some other types of notes that you will encounter:

1. **The Dotted Half Note**
   A dot after the half note increases its value by half. In a $\frac{4}{4}$ time signature, a half note represents two beats, so its dot is worth one beat, making the dotted half note equal to three beats. Example:

   Count out loud while tapping out the note.

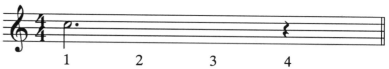

2. **The Triplet**
   In a $\frac{4}{4}$ time signature, a triplet eighth note represents one third of a quarter note and is always found in a group of three eighth notes or eighth rests. Example:

   Count out loud while tapping out the note.

Keys

The key for each study or exercise will be written above it. For the purpose of this book, it is not necessary to have an in-depth knowledge of keys; but if you don't already understand them, you should learn about them.

Chords

All of the chord pictures in this book will be simple, full barre chords and should be fingered exactly as written. When you have completed this book you can experiment with whatever chord voicings and fingerings you like, but for the moment, "Play it as written."

Sight Reading

You do not have to be a good or even an average sight reader to master the material in this book. Indeed, you need only to understand basic rhythms to play all of the exercises. If you are one of the many people who do not read music (including rhythms), then you must develop a methodical approach to each exercise—breaking it down and understanding it theoretically before attempting it practically. If you persist with this method you will gradually take less time to understand each exercise and will always be assured that you are playing exactly what was intended.

Musical Signs

Tie: This adds the duration of the second note to that of the first. The second note is not re-attacked.

Bar Repeat: This sign is placed in a bar that is played exactly as the previous bar.

Repeat Sign: Wherever this sign is placed means that you return to the start of the music or where another sign is found turned in the opposite direction

PRACTICE SCHEDULE

If you have your equipment set up and understand the few rudiments that we have covered, then you should be ready to play!

Practice Schedules

I should like to stress at this point that you practice each and every exercise until it is perfect before commencing with the next. You will need to discipline yourself into a daily practice routine if you wish to make fast progress. Personally, I recommend that you make up a daily practice timetable that is followed rigidly and completed at the end of every day. Make a cassette recording of the day's exercises, which can be analyzed and corrected before the next practice session begins (Fig. 1).

Reggae rhythm guitar, by nature, is technically a relatively simple style. However, it demands great aural awareness and coordination to create subtleties of rhythm, tone, pick stroke, damping, and percussiveness. My advice at this point is:

1. Do not presume or take for granted that you can play any of the exercises until you are sure that you have exhausted every aspect of them.

2. Listen carefully and critically to your own playing. This is the best assurance of consistent progress in a "teach yourself" situation.

Fig. 1

(An example of a practice schedule)

TIME	WORK TO BE DONE
15 Minutes	Listening and analysis of previous day's work tape.
20–30 Minutes	Correct the errors noted from previous day's work.
30–45 Minutes	Read, study, and practice new exercises.
15 Minutes	Record all of the above for analyzing at the next practice session.

DOWN- & UPSTROKES

(THEORY & PRACTICE)

It is assumed that most people using this book have at least a basic knowledge of rudimentary guitar skills. The following exercises are intended for players of all levels to check over and analyze the building blocks of their rhythm technique (down- and upstrokes) to ensure that they understand its proper execution.

LESSON 1: DOWNSTROKE THEORY

The sign ⊓ will indicate where to play a downstroke.

The Right-Hand Movement

The downstroke is controlled from the wrist, with a minimum of movement in the right arm. The pick should go through an oval motion, striking the strings quickly and then completing the rest of the movement at a slower pace. Return to the starting position just as the next chord is to be played (Fig. 2). If a repetitive rhythm is being played, this movement should flow continuously with the rhythm unless there are long rests in between chords.

Because the movement is pivoted at the wrist, the pick will move at a diagonal across the strings (Fig. 3).

Fig. 2:

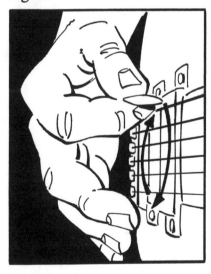

Fig. 3:

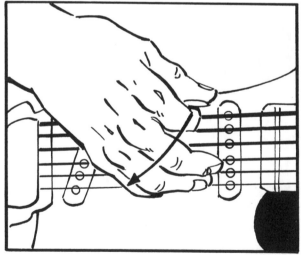

Exercise 1

Practice the downstroke movement using open strings. Watch the movement carefully, using a mirror to ensure that it is as described above.

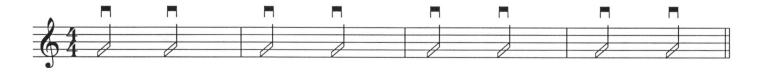

LESSON 2: UPSTROKE THEORY

The sign V will indicate where an upstroke is to be played.

The Movement

The upstroke movement is basically the same as the downstroke except that it is in the opposite direction. It is controlled by the wrist, creating the oval and diagonal motion (Figs. 4 and 5). Strike the strings quickly and then slowly reposition to prepare the pick for the next stroke. The upstroke is always a more difficult stroke to master than the downstroke, so spend extra time practicing it.

Fig. 4:

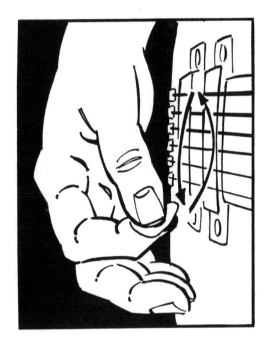

Fig. 5:

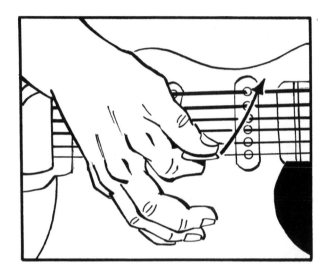

Exercise 2

Practice the upstroke movement using open strings. Watch the right hand carefully, playing slowly at first and gradually increasing the speed. The upstroke has to feel as comfortable to use as the downstroke. When playing the upstroke, all six strings do not have to be played. Start by striking the top three strings, consistently striking the same number for each stroke.

LESSON 3: DOWNSTROKE PRACTICE

New Chords To Be Used

Make sure that you can play the following chords proficiently before attempting Exercise 3.

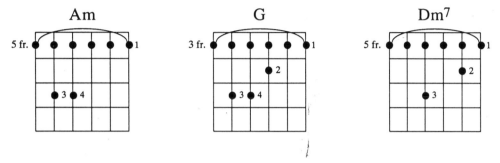

Exercise 3

1. Play the exercise slowly at first, gradually building up the speed.

2. Try to use the same volume and attack for each chord.

3. Initially, count out loud while playing. Try to keep the rhythm as regular and even as possible.

Key: A Minor
Use ⊓ throughout.

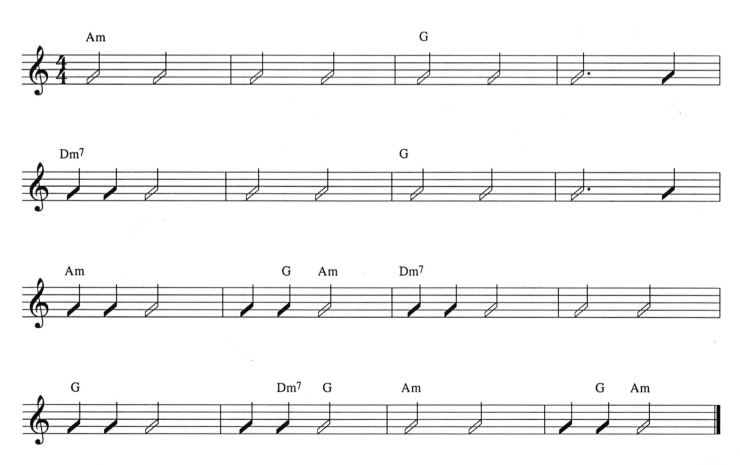

LESSON 4: UPSTROKE PRACTICE

Exercise 4

Try to keep the right hand as relaxed as possible and remember to consider the three points mentioned in Exercise 3.

Upstrokes rarely include more than the top four strings: E, B, G, D. Use only the top three or four strings in this exercise.

Key: A Minor
Use V throughout.

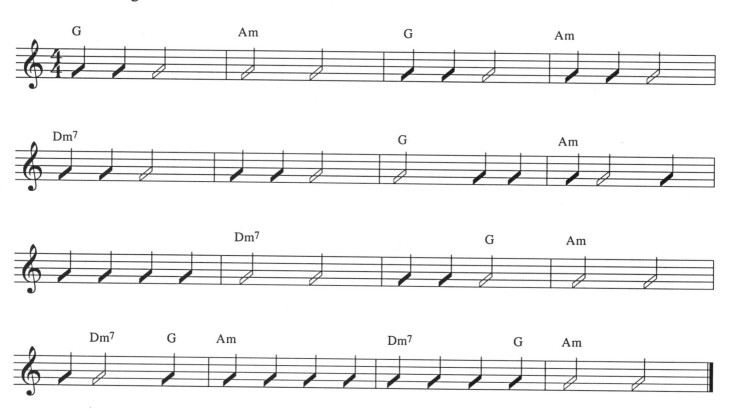

LESSON 5: STROKE CHANGING

In the following exercises you will be playing down- and upstrokes together. When changing from one type of stroke to the other, play only the striking motion of the stroke and then leave the hand in that position ready to play the new stroke; *i.e.*, when changing from a downstroke to an upstroke, play only the striking part of the *downstroke* oval movement. This will leave the hand positioned and ready to play the *upstroke*. Practice this movement before attempting Exercise 5.

New Chords

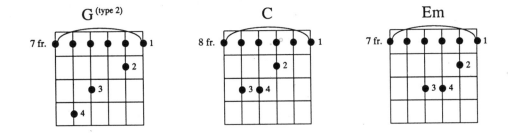

Exercise 5

The following should be played smoothly, with no hesitation between different strokes. Make sure that you can play the new chords with ease. If necessary, count and tap out the rhythms before playing the exercise.

Key: C Major

BASIC TECHNIQUES

LESSON 6: STRING GROUPING

In rhythm playing, any number of strings can be used. A number will be written inside the stroke sign to indicate the number of strings to be struck to create a particular voicing.

The string number inside the stroke sign is always inclusive of the high E (1st string), regardless of which stroke sign is used.

⊓ will indicate to strike the top *four* strings only, using a downstroke. (The stroke will start from the D string – Fig. 6.)

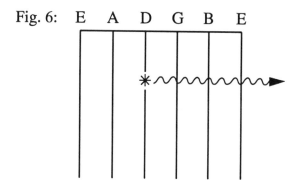

Fig. 6:   E   A   D   G   B   E

V⁴ will indicate to strike the top four strings only using an upstroke. (The stroke will start on the first E string – Fig. 6a.)

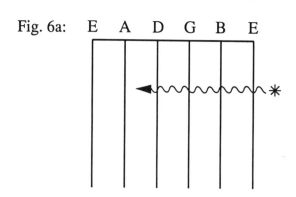

Fig. 6a: E   A   D   G   B   E

Accurate and consistent performance of this technique is essential.

Exercise 6

Practice through the following examples. Play slowly at first, concentrating on accuracy and striking the indicated string groups correctly.

All in Key of A Minor

LESSON 7: DAMPING

After a chord has been struck, its sound will be sustained until it naturally dies away. Damping is the means of controlling the length of the sustain by physically muting the strings. Damping can be done by the left hand or the right hand. In the following exercises you will learn how to damp the strings with either hand to produce *staccato* (short) or *tenuto* (long) sounds.

The Staccato Sound

This is a sound that is held (sustained) for the shortest duration possible. A chord that is played *staccato* is damped immediately after being played. Staccato chords are the most common types of chords found in Reggae. The sign • will be written to show that a chord is to be played staccato.

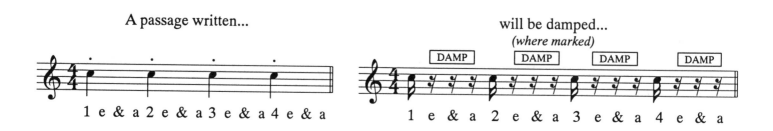

The Tenuto Sound

This is a sound that is held (sustained precisely for its written duration). Damping takes place only to produce rests that fall in between tenuto chords. The sign – will be written to show that a chord is to be played tenuto.

LESSON 8: TENUTO DOWNSTROKES, RIGHT HAND DAMPING

The Movement

The *tenuto downstroke* is played with the normal oval and diagonal downstroke motion, except that:

1. When the pick has completed the oval motion, the strings are damped at the start of the next beat by letting the edge of the palm of the right hand fall onto the strings (Fig. 7). The pick is now prepared for the next stroke as soon as the edge of the palm of the right hand is raised off the strings.

2. After striking the strings, the oval motion should be completed slightly faster than normal to allow enough time to damp the strings precisely on the following beat.

Fig. 7:

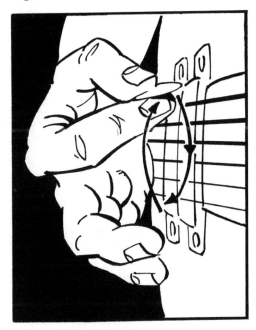

Fig. 8:

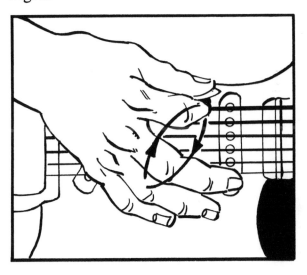

Whenever damping takes place, the edge of the right palm should contact the strings about an inch from the bridge. The edge of the palm will fall across the strings at a diagonal angle because of the position of the hand (Fig. 8). The damping action itself should be gentle but firm, so that it does not produce a clicking sound when the hand comes into contact with the strings.

Exercise 7

Practice the technique described above in the following exercise.

The sign ⊏ written above a chord indicates that it is to be played tenuto and then damped with the right hand.

Exercise 8

Concentrate on producing a steady rhythm with controlled, even movements of the right hand.

Key: A Minor
Use ▯ and ⊏ throughout.

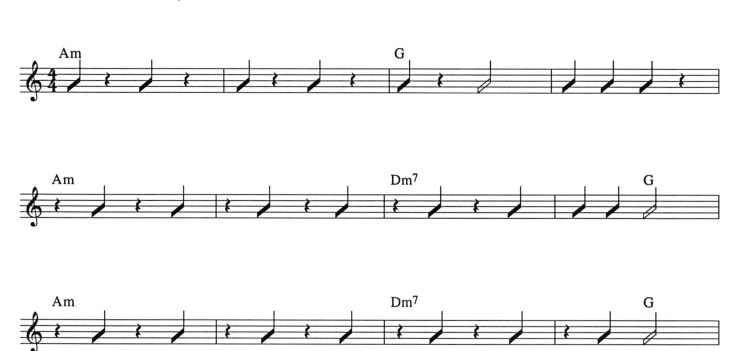

LESSON 9: TENUTO UPSTROKES, RIGHT HAND DAMPING

The normal upstroke movement (Exercise 2) is used to play the tenuto upstroke, except that:

1. To produce the rest after a tenuto chord, the plectrum completes the oval motion and damping is applied by letting the edge of the right palm fall onto the strings (Fig. 9). The pick is now prepared for the next stroke as soon as the edge of the palm is raised off the strings.

2. After striking the strings, the remainder of the upstroke oval motion should be completed slightly faster than normal to allow enough time to execute the damping precisely at the start of the next beat.

The right-hand position should be the same as in Figs. 4 and 5. Remember to keep the damping action gentle but firm to avoid any unwanted clicking sounds.

Fig. 9:

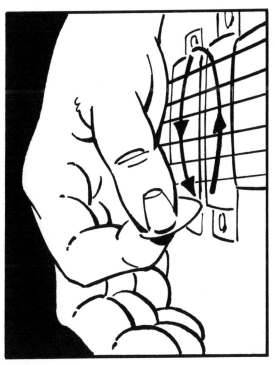

Exercise 9

Practice the technique described above using the following exercise. The upstroke should feel as comfortable and relaxed as the downstroke.

New Chords

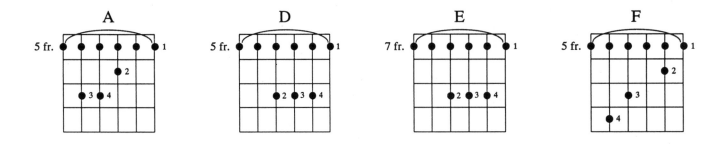

Ensure that you can play the new chords and changes easily before attempting the next exercise.

Exercise 10

The following is played tenuto (each chord is held for its written duration). Play slowly at first. Concentrate on producing a steady rhythm with controlled, even movements of the up-stroke.

Key: A Major
Use ⱽ and ⱻ throughout.

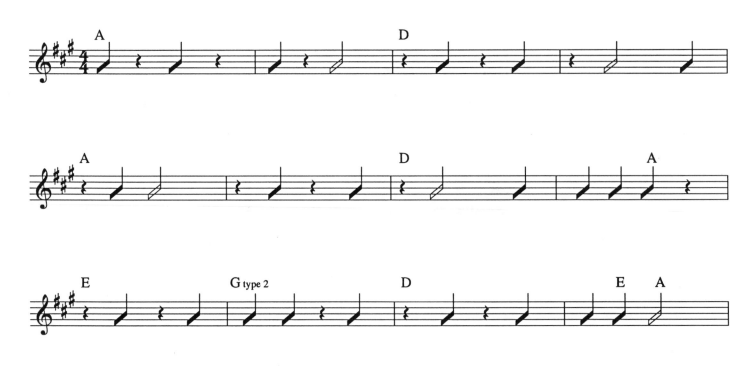

LESSON 10: TENUTO DOWN- & UPSTROKES, RIGHT HAND DAMPING

In the following exercise, remember to use the correct stroke-changing movement (as described in Lesson 5). Make sure that every stroke is tenuto and that damping takes place at the correct time. Pay special attention to the string groupings and make sure they are played accurately.

Exercise 11

Key: A Minor
Use **F** throughout.

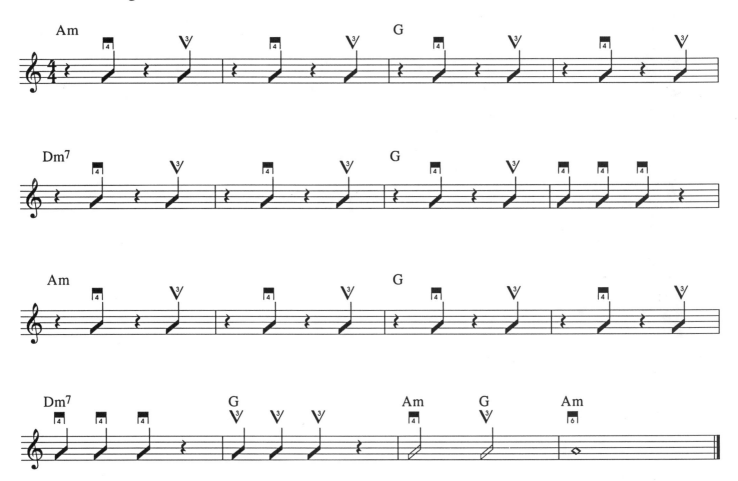

LESSON 11: STACCATO DOWNSTROKES, RIGHT-HAND DAMPING

The *staccato downstroke* is played idfferently than the normal oval-shaped downstroke. Striking the chord is the same as the normal downstroke, but the edge of the palm of the right palm damps the strings as soon as the pick completes the stroke (Fig. 10).

With the edge of the palm still damping the strings, the pick is repositioned for the next downstroke by moving in a V shape, because the edge of the palm remains on the strings (Fig. 11).

The right hand stays in this position ready for the next stroke, releasing the damping just before the next chord is played.

Fig. 10:

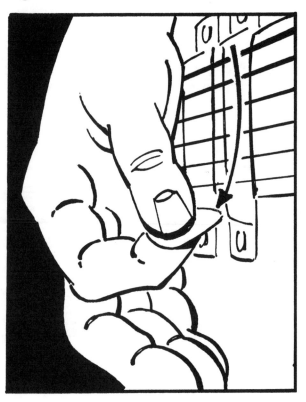

Fig. 11:

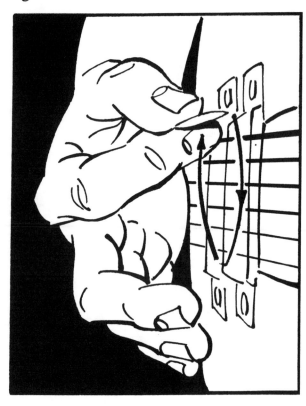

Exercise 12

Play the following exercise using the technique described above. Start off slowly and only increase the speed when your hand is comfortable with the technique.

The sign ⌐ indicates that a chord is to be played staccato by damping with the right hand. Do not let the speed of the damping affect the evenness and flow of the pick strokes. Make sure that you damp the strings until just before the next chord is played.

Exercise 13

Key: C Major
Use ⊓ and ⌐ throughout.

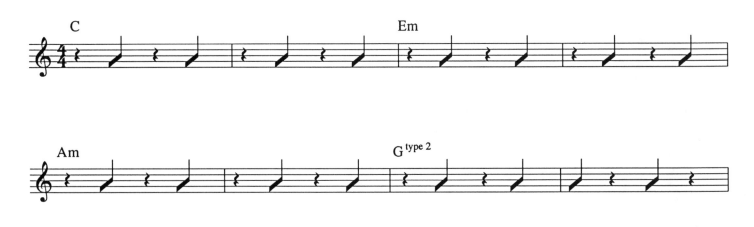

LESSON 12: STACCATO UPSTROKES, RIGHT-HAND DAMPING

Like the staccato downstroke, the upstroke uses a V shaped movement instead of the normal oval movement. As soon as the strings have been struck, the edge of the right palm damps the strings (Fig. 12). Then with the strings still damped, the pick is repositioned, using the V-shaped motion, preparing it for the next stroke (Fig. 13). The hand is now ready to play another stroke as soon as the damping is released.

Fig. 12:

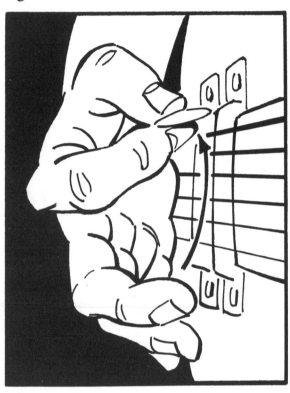

Fig. 13:

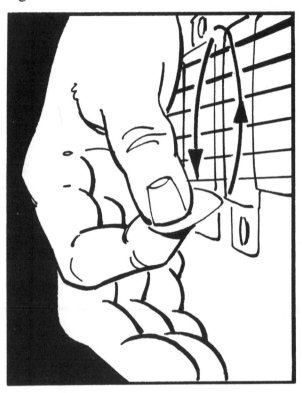

Exercise 14

Play the following exercise with the technique described above until it feels comfortable and relaxed.

Play the following exercise slowly at first, gradually increasing the speed. Concentrate on not letting the damping with the edge of the palm affect the evenness and flow of the pick strokes. Make sure the strings are damped for the correct duration.

Exercise 15

Key: G Major
Use ⌐ and V throughout the exercise.

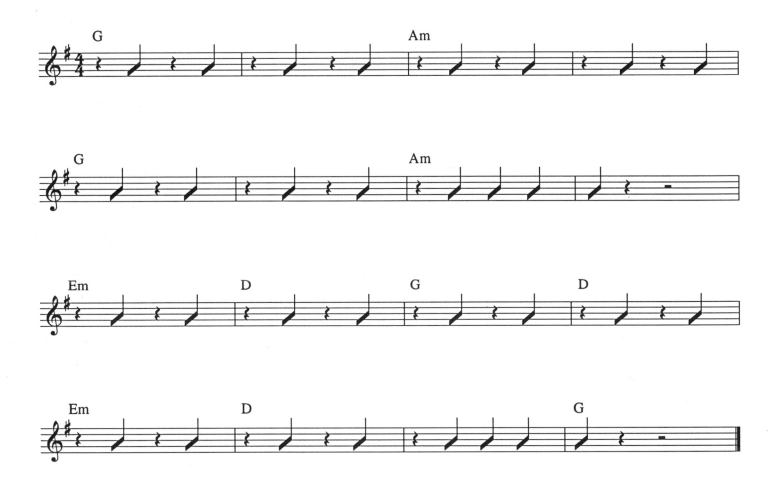

LESSON 13: STACCATO DOWN- AND UPSTROKES, RIGHT-HAND DAMPING

In the following exercise, remember to use the correct stroke-changing movement, as described in Lesson 5. Make sure that every chord is staccato and that the damping creates a consistent sound, regardless of which stroke is used.

Exercise 16

Key: A Minor
Use  throughout.

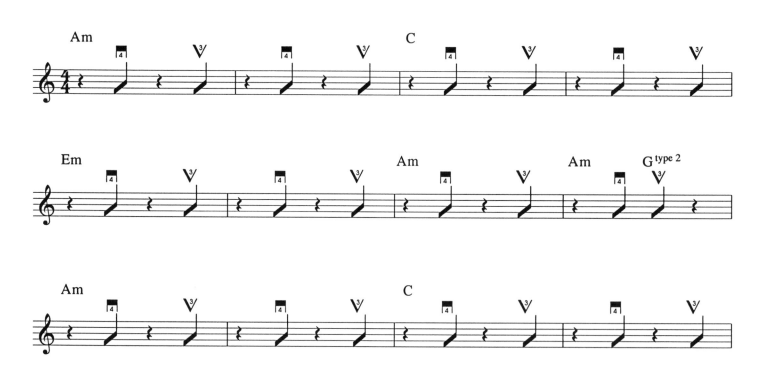

RIGHT-HAND DAMPING SUMMARY POINTS

1. Bring the edge of the right palm into contact with all of the strings simultaneously. This ensures that damping is even and free from buzzing.

2. Always damp all the strings, regardless of how many are played.

3. Relax the middle, ring, and little fingers of the right hand, as in Figs. 7 and 8. Do not let them curl up.

4. Do not let the right-hand fingers and pick drift away from the strings while damping them.

5. Keep movement to a minimum.

Exercise 17: Staccato & Tenuto Down- & Upstrokes

Study the following exercise carefully before playing. Start off slowly, gradually increasing the speed. The changes of stroke direction and damping from staccato to tenuto should sound relaxed and even.

Key: A Major

Use ⌐ throughout.

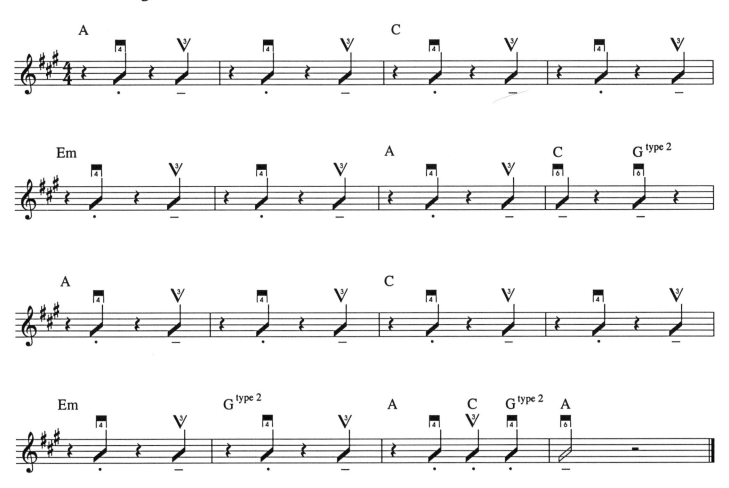

LESSON 14: LEFT-HAND DAMPING

Left-hand damping is an extremely important technique, but relatively easy when compared to right-hand damping.

The Movement

The left hand damps the sound of the strings by releasing the finger pressure on a chord just enough to mute the sound, but without losing contact with the strings. Figure 14 shows the left-hand position as a chord is just about to be played. Figure 15 shows the left-hand position after the chord has been played and damping has taken place. Notice how the fingers have released their pressure on the strings but are still in contact with them.

The pick strokes of the right hand are played as in Lesson 5.

Fig. 14:   Fig. 15:

Important Points to Remember:

1. The left-hand damping technique is the same whether producing staccato or tenuto. The only difference is when to apply the damping.

2. When damping with the left hand, always use a full barre to cover all six strings. This is for two reasons:

   A. To ensure that no discordant open-string tones are produced when a chord is sounded; and

   B. To ensure that all of the sound coming from the guitar is cleanly muted, since the barre finger can release its pressure on all six strings simultaneously.

Exercise 18: Tenuto

The sign ⌐ indicates that a chord is to be played *tenuto* using left-hand damping. Play the following slowly at first, to make sure that you are damping accurately at each rest. Try to keep the right-hand movement even and steady.

Use ⌐ and ⊓ throughout.

Exercise 19: Staccato

The sign ⌐ indicates that a chord is to be played *staccato* using left-hand damping. Play the following slowly and concentrate on producing a short attacking sound consistent in duration and tone.

Use ⌐ and ⊓ throughout.

In the following exercise, be sure to differentiate clearly between the tenuto and staccato sounds. The right hand should be completely independent of the left, and stroke direction changing should not affect the consistency of the rhythm. Pay special attention to the coordination and independence of the hands.

Exercise 20

Key: C Major
Use ⊓ and L throughout unless otherwise indicated.

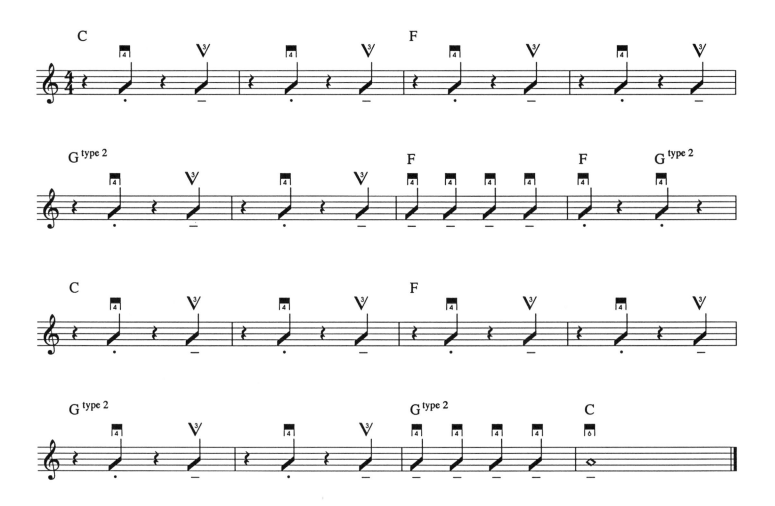

NEW RHYTHMS

LESSON 15: REGGAE BEATS

In the following pages I will be introducing you to examples of traditional Reggae beats. I will suggest damping and chord voicings, but once you become comfortable with the exercises, experiment.

Remember that Reggae is a very "laid-back" style of music and the pulse is never anticipated. Make a habit of listening to the drummer's hi-hat—whether he is playing a "straight eighth" or "triplet" pattern. The hi-hat gives Reggae its feel, and you should always choose the guitar rhythm pattern with it as a reference point.

Exercise 21:   The "One Drop"

This beat can always be recognized by the kick drum and snare (or side stick) playing together on the third pulse of the measure.   The guitar part should not be busy and is normally a staccato stroke on every second and fourth pulse.

Key: A Minor
Use ∟ (lines 1 and 2), and Γ (lines 3 and 4).

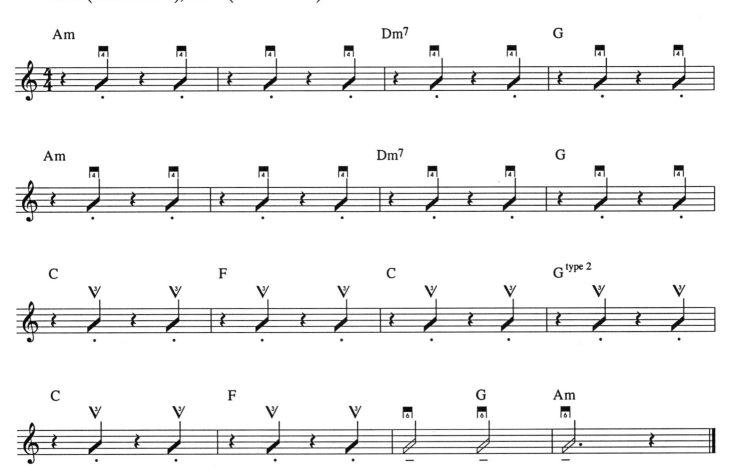

Exercise 22: The "Four Drop," or "Steppers"

This beat can be recognized by the straight pulses of the kick drum on each quarter note of the measure. A wide variety of guitar rhythms can fit over this beat, but the important thing to remember is how the guitar rhythm sits with the bass.

Key: C Major
Use r (lines 1, 2, and 4) and L (line3)

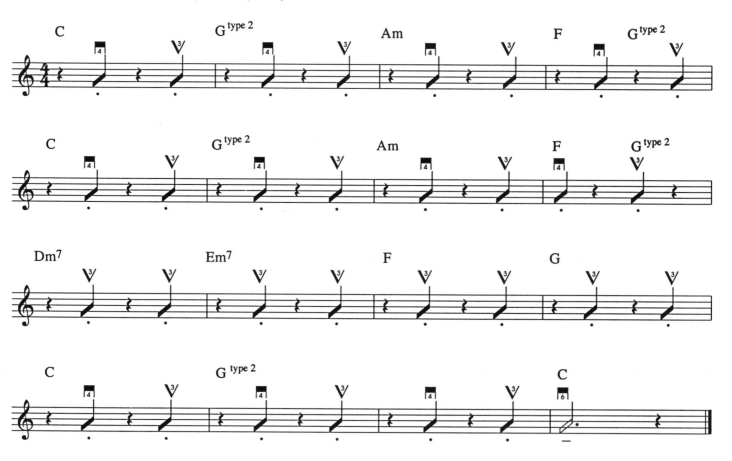

Exercise 23: The "Two Drop"

This beat can be recognized in its simplest form by the kick drum pattern, which plays on the first and third pulses of the measures. There are many derivatives of this beat, and in many cases they are created by adding to the kick drum pattern.

Key: E Minor
Use L throughout.

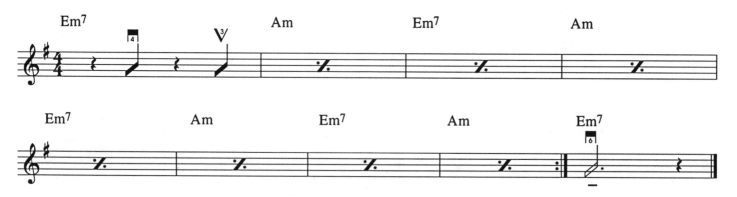

36

LESSON 16: RHYTHM FILLS

The following are techniques for creating chord fills in order to develop interest within the basic rhythm pattern. This effect is usually created by adding a note extension to the chord with the fourth finger.

Check the notation against the tablature and chord picture to ensure that you are playing the right notes. Fills are normally made up of tenuto eighth notes ($\flat$) without damping, except for the last note, which is staccato and damped. Because these fills use eighth notes, count out the bars with:

1 & 2 & 3 & 4 &

Exercise 24: The Minor 7th Fill

Play through the following slowly. Remember that a tied note (⌢) is not played but is still sounded from the previous note.

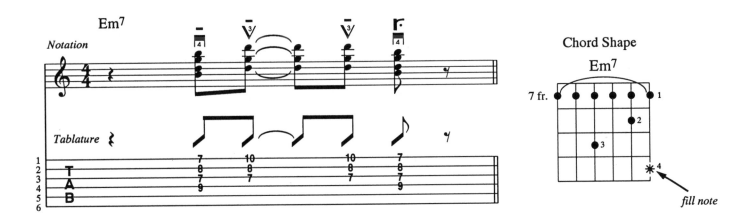

Exercise 25

Play the following:

Key: E Minor
Use **r** throughout.

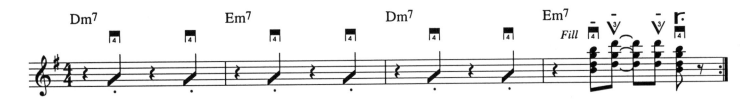

Exercise 26: The Minor 9th Fill

Use the same approach as in Exercise 25. The sixth and fifth strings in the following chord shapes are left open, so strike only the top four strings. Make sure to damp all six strings with the right hand on the last eighth note, to stop any unwanted vibration.

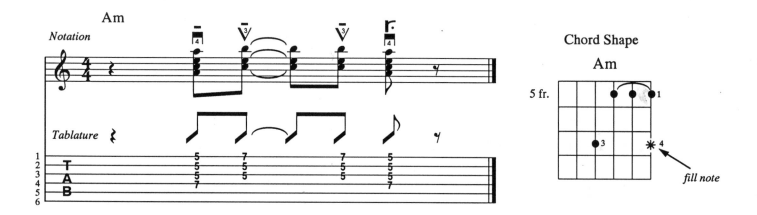

Exercise 27

Key: G Major

Play the following. Use ⊓ and Γ throughout unless otherwise indicated.

Exercise 28: The 9th Fill

Use the same approach as in Exercises 25 and 27. Pay attention to the open sixth and fifth strings.

Chord Shape

A

fill note

Exercise 29

Key: A Major

Play the following. Use ⊓ and ⊓ throughout unless otherwise indicated.

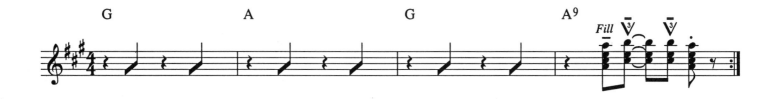

LESSON 17: RHYTHMIC PATTERNS

In this lesson you will find eight new rhythm patterns, consisting of four straight-eighth patterns in Exercise 30 and their triplet-feel (shuffle-feel) counterparts in Exercise 31. Work through them one at a time until you can play them naturally without any hesitation. These patterns are some of the most common in Reggae guitar. After mastering them, you can freely interchange them and experiment to form new patterns.

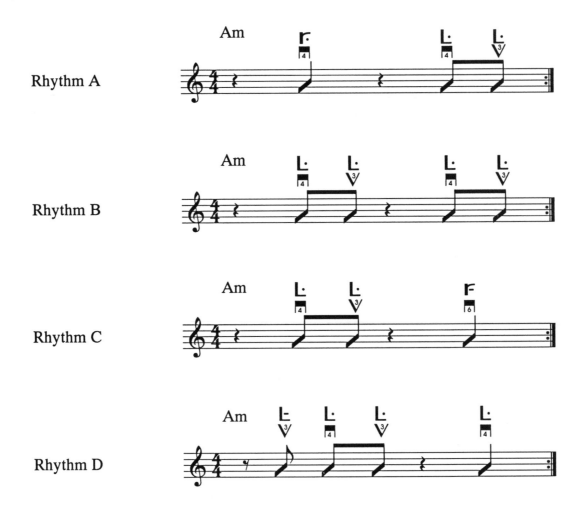

Exercise 30

Play the following carefully using Rhythm patterns A, B, C, and D. Practice them until they feel comfortable and relaxed.

Key: A Minor

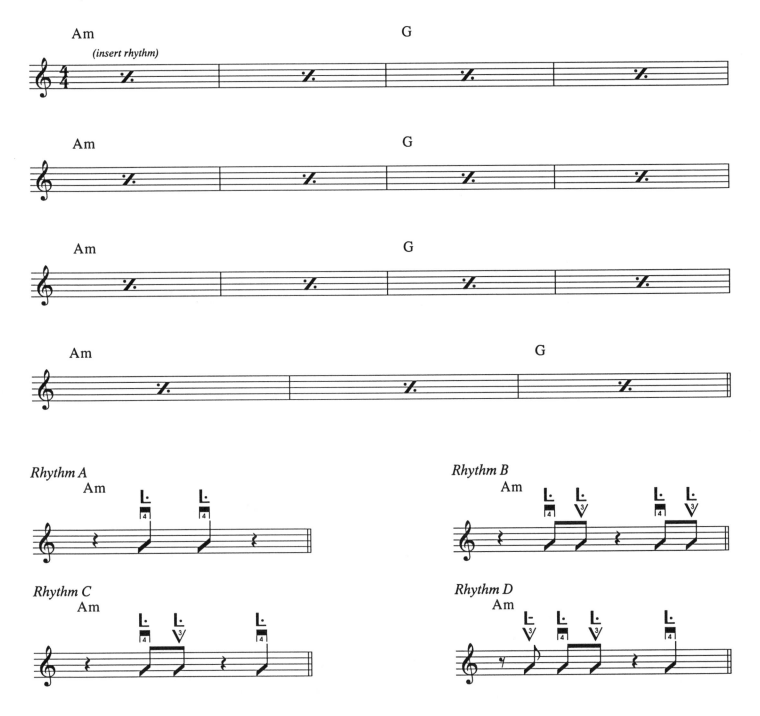

The following rhythm patterns all have a triplet, or shuffle, feel. Try to be as relaxed as possible when playing them. Listen carefully to the bass and hi-hat patterns and let the guitar part "sit down in the rhythm."

The following exercise uses a Cmaj7 chord, which, along with a shuffle feel, is typically found in a style of Reggae called "Lovers Rock."

New Chord

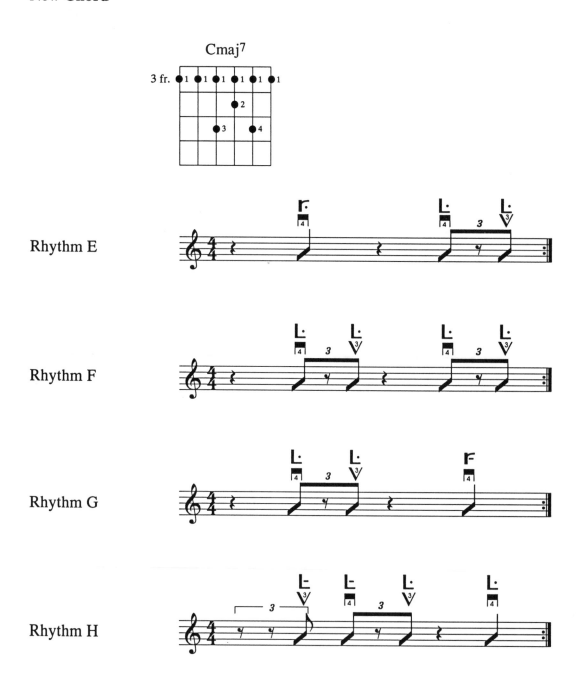

Exercise 31

Play the following carefully using Rhythm patterns E, F, G, and H. Practice them until they feel comfortable and relaxed.

Key: C Major

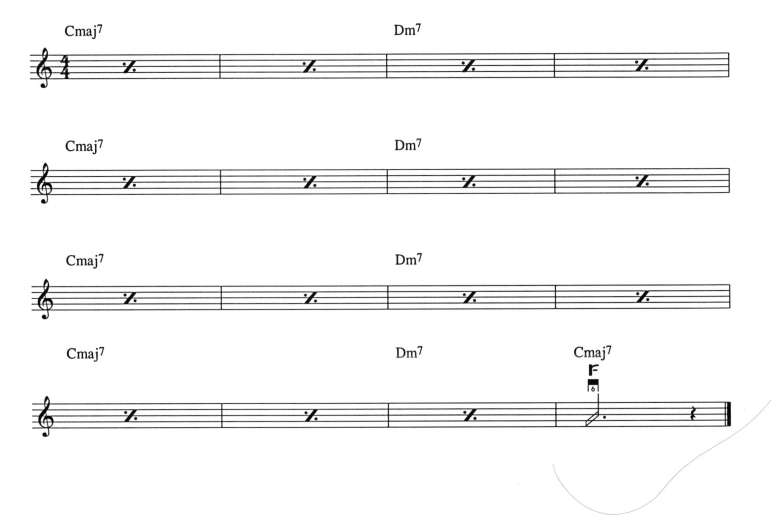

LESSON 18: BEFORE REGGAE

At this point, I would like to put the work that you have covered into perspective by briefly outlining some of the indigenous Jamaican beats that preceded and influenced Reggae. These older rhythms are still very potent and are starting to be re-used by some of the more contemporary composers and producers.

MENTO

Mento is one of the earliest popular Jamaican rhythms and is rooted strongly in traditional folk music. Study the following rhythm structure carefully before attempting the exercise.

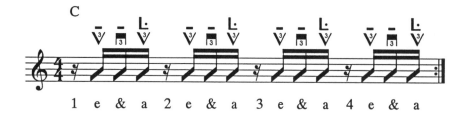

Exercise 32

Key: C Major

SKA

Ska as a rhythm grew out of American Jazz and Blues of the 1950s and started out as an interpretation of that music by Jamaican musicians, who gradually added their own feel and sound.

Study the following rhythm structure carefully before attempting the exercise.

Ska: Straight-eighth feel

Exercise 33

Play as above.

Key: C Major

SKA (BLUE BEAT or SHUFFLE FEEL)

This rhythm is basically the same as the "straight-eighth," except that it is played with a swing, or triplet, feel. Study the structure of Rhythm A carefully before attempting exercise 34. Count the triplet quarter notes "1 & a 2 & a 3 & a 4 & a."

Rhythm A

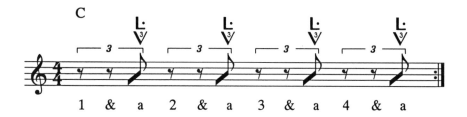

1 & a 2 & a 3 & a 4 & a

Exercise 34

Key: C Major

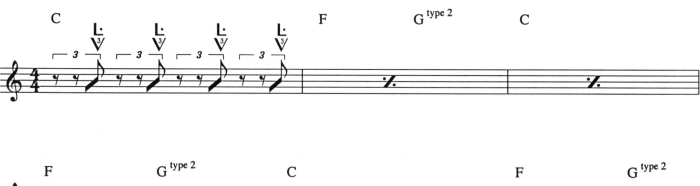

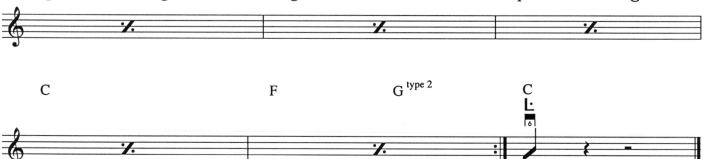

ROCK STEADY

Rock Steady was popular in the mid to late 1960s. As a rhythm it is basically a slow Reggae, typically using the "One Drop" drum beat. Study the structure of Rhythms A and B before attempting Exercise 35.

Rhythm A

Rhythm B

Exercise 35

Play as above.

Key: G Major

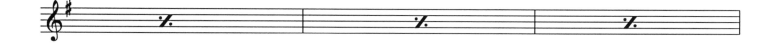

LESSON 19: CHORDS

I have kept the chords used in previous exercises as simple as possible, so that emphasis could be placed on the technique at hand. Now that you have mastered these techniques, it's time to expand your chord usage and knowledge.

A good chord dictionary is always a sound investment. You can get by with a basic knowledge of chords, but a wide chord vocabulary helps to give you control over chord voicings and position playing (a great asset).

Reggae is not a harmonically complex style of music; in most cases, it is quite simple. Therefore, I recommend the following chords as a basic requirement in order to become competent with common keys and progressions.

All of the following chords are chromatic, which means that they can be moved up and down the fingerboard and become a new chord at each fret position. The basic chord type (*e.g.*, maj7) will not change, but the letter designating the chord will. The sign ◉ will be used to mark the tonic note (letter name) of the chord.

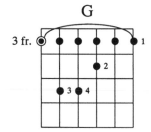
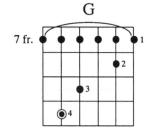
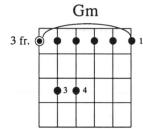
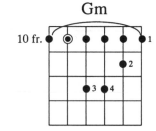

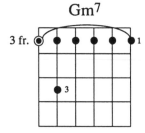
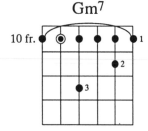
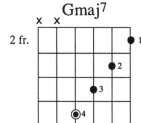
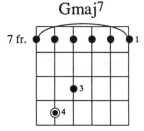

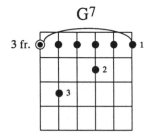
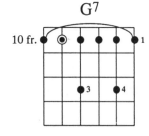
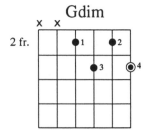
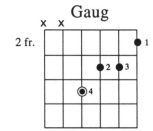

LESSON 20: BASS LINES & RIFFS

Another aspect of Reggae guitar playing that has a fairly important role is that of playing single lines. This can be categorized into two forms: bass lines and riffs.

Bass Lines (Tracking)

This is where the guitar follows what the bass is playing and acts as a doubling instrument.

Riff Playing

This is usually a single melodic figure that is repeated throughout a song, with emphasis being put as much on its rhythmic structure as on its melodic contour.

The Technique and Sound

When playing riffs or bass lines the approach is basically the same:

1. A muted sound is always used on bass lines and usually on riffs. Muting is performed by resting the edge of the palm of the right hand on the strings where they cross the bridge saddles. The right hand remains in this position as the riff or bass line is being played.

2. The right hand position can be moved to change the amount of muting; back toward the bridge reduces the muting, forward toward the fingerboard increases it. The normal position is right on the bridge saddle.

3. Riffs can be played anywhere on the fingerboard. Bass lines are always played on the sixth, fifth, and fourth strings.

4. The tone of the guitar should have an emphasis on mid frequencies. This is normally achieved by using a combination of two pickups, or the center pickup on a three-pickup instrument. Make the sound as "rounded" as possible. Sometimes a compressor can be used to enhance the sound.

The following progression is used in Exercise 36a, b, and c.

Key: C Major

Exercise 36a: Bass Lines

The following melody is the bass line of Exercise 36. Concentrate on tracking the bass as tightly as possible, and try to produce a consistent sound.

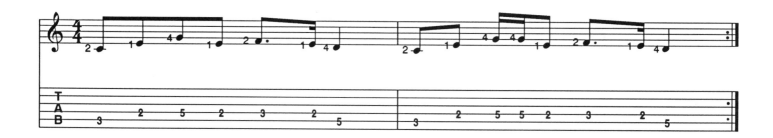

Exercise 36b: Riffs

In the following exercise, note that the riff acts as a counterrhythm to the bass line. It is important that the bass line and riff do not clash. In a standard Reggae rhythm section with two guitars, one would usually play rhythm guitar and the other could play riffs or bass lines.

Study the following carefully before attempting the exercise.

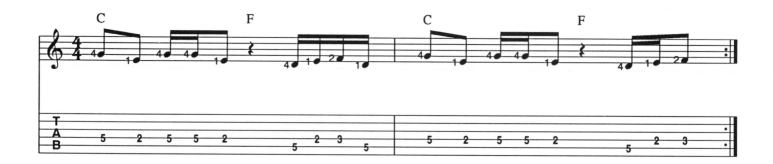

Exercise 36c: The "Rattle"

This is a musical effect normally used in both riffs and bass lines. To achieve the sound, single note in the melody is rhythmically double (*e.g.*, from a single eighth note to double sixteenth notes), or if it's the first note of the phrase, it is given a pickup, usually of two sixteenth notes.

The "rattle" is always used at the player's own discretion and should never be overused or sound predictable.

The following is the same melody as Exercise 36b, but with the "rattle" variations. Study it carefully before attempting Exercise 36c.

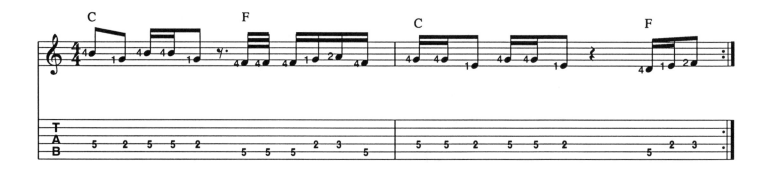

Experiment with the placement of the "rattle" in this exercise as much as you like, but remember that it should sound integrated with the rhythm as a whole and not be overused.

LESSON 21: PERCUSSIVE PLAYING

This is a subtle technique that should add more dynamics and dimension to your playing. When you listen to recordings of good Reggae guitarists, you will notice that their overall sound can vary from an almost unpitched percussive sound to a very clear and sustained ring. I am using the word *percussive* to describe the sound when it has lost its ring (sustain). The following exercise will demonstrate.

Exercise 37

The effect is achieved by varying the pressure of the left-hand fingers when holding a chord. Less finger pressure produces less sustain and more percussiveness. The real difficulty is to keep the pressure consistent, so that one continuous sound is produced. This technique can be used with either left- or right-hand damping, and you should be able to create at least three distinct sounds.

Play through the following. Note that the first bar is played with normal left-hand pressure, which is reduced in the second and third bars to create increasingly percussive sounds. After mastering the exercise, try playing through some of the previous staccato exercises using one of these sounds at a time. When playing with tenuto, use of this technique is limited because it interferes with the duration of the sound.

LESSON 21: PERCUSSIVE PLAYING

A *dummy stroke* is when the right hand produces a down- or upstroke movement *without actually striking the strings*. The purpose of this is to tighten up the timing by doubling the right-hand tempo, but this can only be employed when left-hand damping is used. In effect, the right hand makes two strokes for every single stroke that is heard.

In the following musical example, the dummy strokes are used on any rest that comes after a playing stroke. Note that the first stroke is always a playing stroke at the start of a progression, after which the dummy strokes are used. The dummy stroke does not have to be a complete stroke motion, but can be used as if only the three lower strings for downstrokes or three upper strings for upstrokes are being played. Remember that this technique is intended to improve your timing, so practice it carefully with this goal in mind.

Play the following slowly at first and gradually increase the tempo. When it feels comfortable, try using this technique on some of the earlier exercises.

"D" indicates where to play the dummy stroke.

LESSON 23: SOUND EVALUATION

Something you must always remember when working through a book such as this is that you are teaching yourself, and so you should try to be as objective as possible about your playing. To do this, it is helpful to have a consistent and regularly used evaluating system that will help to question and analyze various aspects of your playing.

The table below can be used as such and is intended to help remind you of some of the most obvious components that, together, make up your sound and technique. I have broken these down into three basic groups:

    a. Technical
    b. Electrical
    c. Mechanical

Use a recorded exercise of yourself and listen to it carefully, going through each group item by item, asking yourself the following questions:

    1. Can I, and am I, controlling this aspect of my sound?
    2. Do I have enough control over this aspect to produce the sound I want?
    3. In which area is this aspect most lacking?
    4. What can I do to improve this aspect:
        a. immediately; and
        b. in the long term?

TECHNICAL	ELECTRICAL	MECHANICAL
Damping	Pickup Sound	String Action
String Grouping	Amp Tone	Pick Thickness
Down- and Upstrokes	Guitar Tone	Pick Size
Force of Pick Stroke	Effects	Intonation
Stroke Consistency		Pickup Adjustment
Percussiveness		String Gauge

You should find the list above helpful in forming an objective opinion about your own playing. I suggest that you use this evaluation system once a week and keep a written record of your conclusions. You will then be able to study your rate of improvement over a period of time and see which areas present the greatest difficulties.

CONCLUSION

I hope you have found this book helpful to your playing and, if so, achieved a firmer grasp of Reggae guitar. I must stress, however, that the book is not an end in itself, but a supplement to go with listening to and playing as much Reggae music as possible. Try to be objective about your own playing and never be afraid to experiment and try new ideas. After all, that's how we keep moving forward.